To Kate – BB
To my mother and father – CB

The author and illustrator acknowledge with thanks the generous help offered
by the Institut Pasteur in Paris, and especially Mlle Chardon, whose assistance
has been invaluable.

The illustrator would also like to thank Tamsyn Barker for all her help.

First published in Great Britain 1995
by Victor Gollancz
A Division of the Cassell group
Wellington House, 125 Strand, London WC2R 0BB

Text copyright© Beverley Birch 1995
Illustrations copyright© Christian Birmingham 1995

Edited by Belinda Hollyer
Designed by Herman Lelie
Produced by Mathew Price Ltd
The Old Glove Factory, Bristol Road, Sherborne
Dorset DT9 4HP, England

The right of Beverley Birch and Christian Birmingham to be
identified as authors of this work has been asserted by them in
accordance with the Copyright, Designs and Patents Act, 1988

A catalogue record for this book is
available from the British Library

ISBN 0 575 06014 X

Printed in Hong Kong

PASTEUR'S
FIGHT AGAINST MICROBES

Beverley Birch
Illustrated by Christian Birmingham

VICTOR GOLLANCZ
LONDON

The father looked at the teacher. Would he help?

The teacher looked at the father. He did not want to say no. He did not want to disappoint the father of one of his pupils.

But how could he possibly help? What did he, a science teacher, know about turning beetroots into alcohol?

But the father was looking at him so hopefully. Surely (his gaze seemed to say) you will come and look. You, Monsieur Pasteur, have set the boys of our city of Lille on fire with your fascinating lessons about the wonders of the natural world.

Surely you, of all people, can solve our terrible problem at the sugarbeet factory?

Troubled, Monsieur Pasteur allowed the father to lead him into the factory, between the great vats of foaming sugarbeet juice.

Cautiously Monsieur Pasteur peered in.

The liquid had a heady smell, strong and vinegary, with a rich undercurrent of sweetness. The father, Monsieur Bigo, showed him proudly – here they fermented sugarbeet grown in the surrounding fields of northern France. That was a good fermentation, making fine alcohol.

But look at this! Pasteur leaned across, curious, and drew back in sudden shock. The smell was foul. Sour. The liquid oozed with an evil-looking grey slime. Something was going dreadfully wrong in this vat.

So this was Monsieur Bigo's problem!

It was happening all over the factory, Monsieur Bigo explained. So much time wasted! So much money lost! And all because some sugarbeet was turning to slime, instead of to alcohol.

What was wrong? Full of hope, Monsieur Bigo waited for Pasteur's answer.

Pasteur was silent. It was no good saying there wasn't even the beginnings of a helpful idea in his head. He must try to help.

But where could he start? Monsieur Bigo was pinning all hope on Pasteur because Pasteur was a scientist. Yet he wasn't a scientist who knew how to make juice ferment into alcohol!

Still, Pasteur reminded himself, scientists always have a good long look at things before they find their answers. So, first, look at some of the sour mess ...

He ladelled some into a bottle. Then, to make sure he did look at everything, he put some of the good fermentation into another bottle, and away he carried them to his laboratory.

He sniffed at both bottles. He held them up to the light. He looked at them from every angle.

Neither bottle gave him a single clue.

Perhaps have a closer look, with a microscope? A lens to enlarge his view of the liquid might show him something he couldn't see now.

He put a drop of the good stuff on to a glass slide and slipped it below the lens. Then he leaned forward to stare through the eyepiece at the tiny pool.

It swam!

Pasteur blinked. Carefully he adjusted the eyepiece and put his eye to it again.

Now he could see it wasn't the pool that was swimming – there were things in it. Tiny – yellowish, round, oval – and darker dots swarmed inside them.

The little drop was brimful!

What were they? Desperately he searched his memory, poking into odd corners of his mind where he stored snippets from his reading ...

Yeasts. The name popped suddenly to the front of his mind. That's what they were! Whenever juices were fermenting into alcohol, these tiny shapes were also in the liquid: yeasts.

But what were they doing? How they twirled and sailed – they looked alive, toiling, travelling – in bunches, chains, alone ...

He remembered reading that one scientist thought yeasts were alive, and another had seen tiny buds sprouting. He put his eye to the microscope. Yes, there were the buds ...

Minutes ticked by. He had a rest, and came back to watch again.

Minutes became an hour ...

Was he imagining it, or was one bud bigger than last time he looked at it?

And another, swelling! And before his disbelieving eyes, the bud broke away.

One round yellow yeast had become two round yellow yeasts.

Suddenly an idea was firm in his mind. The yeasts *were* alive. They were tiny creatures, feeding off the beet-juice, growing, and then splitting to make still more yeasts.

And as they fed, they were making the alcohol.

This business of fermenting juice into alcohol was a giant's work – but it was done by armies of miniature living creatures!

Pasteur shook his head clear of mounting excitement. He must think very carefully. This still didn't explain Monsieur Bigo's sour-smelling, sick vats.

Back to the microscope he went. Now, a drop of the slimy liquid on to a glass slide and under the lens.

No yellow yeasts. He had a careful look over every part of the drop. Not one single round yellow shape. He held the bottle of sour liquid to the light. There *were* specks floating and stuck to the walls of the bottle.

He checked the healthy fermentation.

No specks.

He fetched a long, fine needle and fished around in the bottle of sour stuff. With some effort he managed to lift one grey speck on the tip, then lowered it into a drop of clean water on a glass slide. Carefully he put the slide under the microscope and settled with his eye to the eyepiece.

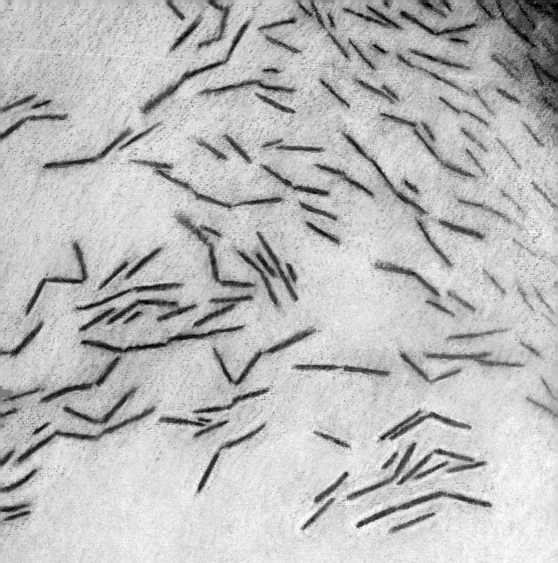

He froze in surprise. The tiny speck was a vast shimmering world of black rods. Millions! All drifting and swirling in a strange, vibrating dance.

Much smaller than the yeasts!

Anxiously he put some healthy fermentation under the microscope. Yeasts again.

No black rods.

Back to the factory he hurried. More bottles
of sour stuff he ladelled up. Back to his
microscope. Drop by drop, on to glass slides
and under the lens it went.

Yes! Whenever it was sour, the dancing black
rods were in it. The sourer it was, the more
black rods there were. And when the rods were
there, there was never any alcohol.

Now he understood. These little black rods were also alive. They had conquered the yeasts and stopped them making alcohol.

Instead, the black rods were making something that turned the liquid sour.

But – just to be sure – more bottles from Monsieur Bigo's factory, more drops of sick stuff, more hours bent over the microscope ...

Until finally he had no doubt. Every time the liquid was sour, the black rods were there. And there was no alcohol, only the acid of sour milk.

He had found the answer to Monsieur Bigo's problem. He couldn't say how the rods got into the vats. But he could tell Monsieur Bigo to check liquid from every vat under a microscope, and if they found one single black rod – even one – they must throw all the liquid away.

If they didn't, that single rod would become millions and kill the yeasts.

As if a war had been fought and won.

He had to return to teaching the boys of Lille. But as the months went by he couldn't forget the little creatures in the sugarbeet vats.

Pasteur was not the first to fall under their spell. Scientists had known about tiny living beings called microbes for two hundred years – since a man peering through a magnifying lens into rainwater first saw them wiggling. But no one knew what they were doing with their never-ending, busy movement.

And now there were pictures rampaging through Pasteur's mind: of yeasts battling to death with black rods: of yeasts making alcohol, and rods making the acid of sour milk.

He must learn more about them! He must grow the black rods in clear liquid, so he could watch them easily. There must be food for them. Perhaps they ate the sugar in beetjuice? Eagerly he mixed sugar and water, and lowered some rods in.

The black rods refused to grow.

He cooked vegetable soup and strained it.

The black rods refused to grow.

He stewed other vegetables, meats ...
anything he could think of, mixing, straining,
boiling till they were free of other microbes.

The rods didn't like any of them.

What else?

Yeasts? He cooked yeasts in water and
added sugar: he fished up a grey speck from a
sour bottle and dropped it into a glass flask of
yeast soup. He sealed the flask and put it
carefully in an oven to keep it at the right
temperature for the rods to grow – not too hot,
not too cold, just gently warm.

Back he went to his teaching.

Every few hours he hurried to the oven and peeped. The yeast soup sat clear, unchanged.

More lessons, more peeps. Still nothing to see.

The day went by, and the next day, filled with lessons and visits from farmers and factory owners of Lille, who all wanted Monsieur Pasteur's help because he was the science teacher who had solved the mystery of the sugarbeet vats for them.

But whenever he could snatch a moment, he peeped some more at his yeast soup in the oven. Still nothing was happening. He began to fear the soup would be just another failure.

At the next chance he took the flask from the oven for a longer look. He was about to put it back, disappointed, when he stopped.

Twirls and curls in the liquid!

He took a closer look. Bubbles puffing upwards.

Gently he lifted the flask to the light. The bubbles came from the speck he'd dropped in the liquid.

He looked again. There were several specks.

But he'd only put *one* in.

Excited, he put a drop under the microscope.

Millions of new black rods. And – he checked very carefully – the acid of sour milk.

Slowly now! No mistakes, no wild guesses. He mixed fresh yeast soup, put new rods in, saw the rods grow ... Again and again he repeated the experiment, until he was sure: the creatures were causing the sourness. They were making the acid of sour milk.

And, if black rods made the sour milk acid, perhaps other tiny creatures in the world were busy making other things! Ideas brimmed in his head: scientists thought microbes were found on rotting things because rotting caused microbes to spring into life. But perhaps it was the other way round! Perhaps rotting happened because *microbes made it happen*.

Months went by. Pasteur moved to Paris, his mind still buzzing. Where did microbes come from? The air? How to find out? He poured yeast soup into flasks, boiled them to kill microbes, melted the flask-necks closed. Then he broke the necks of some of the flasks. Air rushed in. He melted each neck closed again.

The other flasks he never opened. He put them all in his oven, and waited.

In flasks never opened, not *one* microbe grew.

In flasks he did open, microbes grew merrily. Milk, blood, other liquids – it was always the same: if he let air in, microbes came too.

No air, no microbes.

But was it air itself, or dust in the air that brought them? How to let air into his flasks without dust? He wrestled on and on with the problem ...

A scientist friend, peering over Pasteur's shoulder, had an idea. Fill a flask with soup, he said. Then heat and bend the neck to a long S-shape, like a swan's neck. As liquid boils, air will force out of this neck. As liquid cools, air will flow in again, but dust will stick in the bends.

Carefully Pasteur heated and curved the flask necks. Then he waited.

Not one microbe entered the soup. But when he tipped the microbe-free soup into the swan-neck to rinse trapped dust back into the flask, then microbes appeared, growing energetically.

New ideas came to him thick and fast. Firstly, if microbes do travel in dust, he thought, then there will be more microbes where there is more dust. Secondly, there are different amounts of dust in the air in different places: more in a town street, with horses, carts and people moving, than on a high mountain.

By now Pasteur had other scientists helping him with his explorations. Busily they all set to work, preparing flasks of microbe-free yeast soup. Weeks and weeks they spent mixing and boiling them, sealing them, packing them carefully for their journeys.

First, open some in the cellars of a building in Paris. Damp and undisturbed, there would not be much dust moving, and – if Pasteur was right – not many microbes.

Ten flasks were held up, and ten necks snapped off. Air rushed in. Then Pasteur quickly melted the necks with a flame, closing them again.

One flask opened in that cellar grew microbes. Nine flasks remained gloriously microbe-free.

They climbed the stairs to the yard outside, into the bustle of horses, carriages and people. More dust here, thought Pasteur. More microbes.

Ten more flasks were raised, opened, and closed again.

Every one of them grew armies of microbes, multiplying furiously.

Now for a high hill in the country – quieter, cleaner, without the busy movement of a town. Some microbes, thought Pasteur, but not as many as in the street. They snapped the necks off twenty flasks there.

Only eight grew microbes. The other twelve stayed clear.

And on another hill, higher, with cleaner air, they opened twenty more. Only five of those grew microbes. Fifteen stayed clear.

Now they were ready to take their flasks on the longest journey of all. Twenty flasks – packed and loaded on the train. Across France to the mountains of the Alps, they chugged towards the final stage in the adventure begun in the dank cellar in Paris.

They began their climb from the village of Chamonix at the foot of Mont Blanc. Mountain guides led the way on the steep rocky track, then a mule, swaying with flasks slung in cradles across its back. Then Pasteur and his helpers, toiling upwards towards the snowy peaks ahead, squinting through blinding snow-glare, on and up and on and up – until at last they stepped out on the glinting sweep of a great glacier – Mer de Glace, the Sea of Ice.

Here they would perform the final test.

Pasteur lit the torch, with its fierce blue flame.
He took one flask from its cradle on the mule's
back and held it high.

Snap! The steel pincers broke the fine glass
neck. Hiss! Mountain air rushed into the
plump belly of the flask. Then he ran the flame
to and fro across the broken neck, melting it
closed.

On to the next flask, and the next, one after
the other, twenty held up, snapped open,
closed, then nursed all the way back on the
train to the cosy oven in Paris.

Nineteen of the mountain flasks never grew
a single microbe. Only one did.

For eight years Pasteur had explored the microbes' world; he knew they were giants in their work – doing a thousand important tasks.

One enormous question still loomed: what other work was also theirs – dangerous work – killer work? Were microbes at the heart of the mystery puzzling scientists – diseases rampaging across countries, killing hundreds of thousands of people every year? Did microbes invade mouths, noses, ears, grow in people and animals, weaken them, and kill?

It was time to tell the world, and so he called an audience in Paris. He plunged the hall into darkness. Then a beam of light cut the gloom, and in its ray millions of dust specks swirled. Slowly Pasteur began to talk of all the microbes floating there, and of what he knew of their story ...

It was like a gate thrown open, calling scientists to pass through. Find the lurking microbes of disease, urged Pasteur! Learn to stop them, and save millions of lives!

Scientists heard Pasteur's call. His vision came true, and most of us are alive today because of it. And it all began nearly 140 years ago, when a picture gripped a teacher's mind – of rods and yeasts doing battle for Monsieur Bigo's sugarbeet vats ...

When Louis Pasteur began his exploration of the
rotten sugarbeet in 1856, he also began to transform
our world.

Today, we know that there are tiny living creatures
called microbes. They are all around us: in soil,
and in dust that floats in the air and water. Some
microbes do important work, such as helping our
bodies to digest food. But microbes can also
overwhelm a person, an animal or a plant –
and kill it.

Before Pasteur, scientists did not know any of that.
Whole families died of diseases like cholera, typhoid
and bubonic plague. Mothers died having babies,
and children died from pneumonia, tuberculosis,
and diptheria.

Doctors did not know why those things happened.
But after Pasteur's work, they knew that microbes
caused all those deaths. Once that was understood,
doctors and scientists could discover how to prevent
microbes from invading a person's body.

We still use Pasteur's method of heating food and
milk just enough to kill microbes, and we have
named that method after him. It is called
pasteurization.

Pasteur also developed vaccination, later in his life.
This puts weak microbes – called a vaccine – into
your body. Vaccination trains your body to fight the
microbes, so that it learns how to defeat the strong
microbes that cause disease. Today, we have
vaccines against all the diseases that used to kill
people in Pasteur's time. We also have powerful
anti-microbe drugs, called antibiotics.

So most of the diseases which are caused by
microbes can now be defeated, because of the work
that Louis Pasteur began nearly 140 years ago.

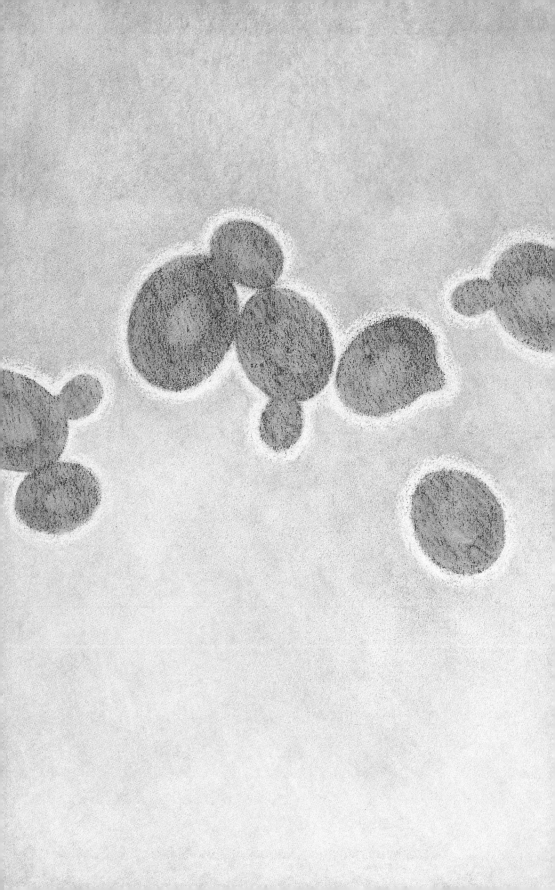